GW00384076

British Library Cataloguing in Publishing Data
A catalogue record of this book is available from the British Library.
ISBN: 978-0-9930201-2-4

Title:	The Key to a Successful Day
Author:	MRDF
Print Size:	Large Booklet

Third Edition 1st of Sha'ban 1436 corresponding to 19th of May 2015

Cover Design:	McCreative
Design & Typesetting:	McCreative

Fig Tree Publications
56 Greenfield Road
London
E1 1EJ
info@figtreepublications.co.uk
www.figtreepublications.co.uk

Fig Tree Publications is a project of the Muslim Research & Development Foundation

Charity no.1119977

INTRODUCTION

فَٱذۡكُرُونِيٓ أَذۡكُرۡكُمۡ وَٱشۡكُرُواْ لِي وَلَا تَكۡفُرُونِ ﴿١٥٢﴾

"So remember Me; I will remember you. And be grateful to Me and do not deny Me."

(2:152)

ٱلَّذِينَ ءَامَنُواْ وَتَطۡمَئِنُّ قُلُوبُهُم بِذِكۡرِ ٱللَّهِۗ أَلَا بِذِكۡرِ ٱللَّهِ تَطۡمَئِنُّ ٱلۡقُلُوبُ ﴿٢٨﴾

"Those who have believed and whose hearts are assured by the remembrance of Allāh . Unquestionably, by the remembrance of Allāh hearts are assured."

(13:28)

وَٱذۡكُر رَّبَّكَ فِي نَفۡسِكَ تَضَرُّعٗا وَخِيفَةٗ وَدُونَ ٱلۡجَهۡرِ مِنَ ٱلۡقَوۡلِ بِٱلۡغُدُوِّ وَٱلۡأٓصَالِ وَلَا تَكُن مِّنَ ٱلۡغَٰفِلِينَ ﴿٢٠٥﴾

"And remember your Lord within yourself in humility and in fear without loudness in words - in the mornings and the evenings. And do not be among the heedless." (7:205)

Remembering Allāh ﷻ is the nourishment for the soul of the believer without which he cannot do. It is also a means to accumulate a tremendous amount of reward. Therefore, a believer should remember Allāh ﷻ as much as he can every day.

The Prophet ﷺ said: "Shall I not inform you of the best of your actions which are the purest to your Lord, which exalt you to the high ranks, which are more efficacious than spending gold and silver (in charity), and better for you than you should encounter your enemies whom you will smite their necks and they will smite your necks?" They said, "Certainly." He ﷺ said, "Remembrance of Allāh the Exalted."

(al-Tirmidhī)

This booklet contains some of the important words of remembrance that we are encouraged to say in the mornings and in the evenings. The morning referred to, is from dawn-break up to when the Sun has risen at the forenoon this may further be extended to the noon prayer. The best time for the evening remembrances is from the 'Aṣr prayer until the Sun has set with the time extended to reaching the first part of the night.

1st Sha'bān, 1436AH
Fig Tree Publications

WHAT TO SAY AFTER THE OBLIGATORY PRAYERS

The Prophet Muḥammad ﷺ related that Allāh عز وجل ordered Yaḥyā ibn Zakariyya with five commandments; to act upon them and convey them to the children of Isrā'īl...(the fifth one being): "...And I order you to make mention of Allāh often, as this is like a man being pursued at speed by the enemy until he reaches a protected fortress and so protects himself inside it, likewise is the servant, he can only protect himself from shaytan through remembrance of Allāh, the Mighty and Majestic "I am with my servant as long as he remembers Me"

Related in Sunan al-Tirmidhī, Sunan al-Nasā'ī & Musnad Aḥmad

The words of remembrance related in this booklet must be recited in Arabic. They are to be recited once only unless otherwise stated.

WHAT TO SAY AFTER THE OBLIGATORY PRAYERS

أَسْتَغْفِرُ اللهَ.

Astaghfirullāh.

I ask for Allāh's forgiveness.

اللّٰهُمَّ أَنْتَ السَّلَامُ وَمِنْكَ السَّلَامُ، تَبَارَكْتَ يَا ذَا الْجَلَالِ وَالْإِكْرَامِ.

Allāhumma antas-Salāmu wa minkas-salāmu, tabārakta yā dhal-Jalāli wal-Ikrām.

O Allāh, You are the Perfect Peace and peace comes from You. Blessed are You, O Owner of majesty and honour.

BENEFITS

Seeking forgiveness is not just done after committing a sin, but also due to one's shortcomings in fulfilling the rights of Allāh ﷻ, such as the deficiencies in the offering of prayers.

As-Salām means the one who is free from deficiencies & imperfections. Note, how we use this name of Allāh ﷻ after performing a prayer which undoubtedly has deficiencies.

NOTES

Repeat 1. *three times*

1. & 2. Related in Ṣaḥīḥ Muslim

BENEFITS

al-Khaṭṭābī رَحِمَهُ اللهُ said: "The essence of supplication is a person displaying his dire need of Allāh whilst realising the basic truth that he has no power or ability to change (anything by himself). This is the mark of true servitude..."

لَا إِلَهَ إِلَّا اللهُ وَحْدَهُ لَا شَرِيكَ لَهُ، لَهُ الْمُلْكُ وَلَهُ الْحَمْدُ وَهُوَ عَلَى كُلِّ شَيْءٍ قَدِيرٌ، اللَّهُمَّ لَا مَانِعَ لِمَا أَعْطَيْتَ، وَلَا مُعْطِيَ لِمَا مَنَعْتَ، وَلَا يَنْفَعُ ذَا الْجَدِّ مِنْكَ الْجَدُّ.

Lā ilāha illallāhu waḥdahū lā sharīka lahū, lahul-mulku wa lahul-ḥamdu wa Huwa `alā kulli shay'in Qadīr. Allāhumma lā māni'a limā a'ṭayta wa lā mu'ṭiya limā mana`ta, wa lā yanfa`u dhal-jaddi minkal-jadd.

None has the right to be worshipped but Allāh alone who has no partner. His is the dominion and to Him belongs all praise; He has power over all things. O Allāh, none can withhold what You give, and none can give what You have withheld; and no wealth or majesty can benefit anyone, as from You is all wealth and majesty.

NOTES

3. Related in Ṣaḥīḥ al-Bukhārī & Ṣaḥīḥ Muslim

لَا إِلَهَ إِلَّا اللهُ وَحْدَهُ لَا شَرِيكَ لَهُ، لَهُ الْمُلْكُ وَلَهُ الْحَمْدُ وَهُوَ عَلَى كُلِّ شَيْءٍ قَدِيرٌ، لَا حَوْلَ وَلَا قُوَّةَ إِلَّا بِاللهِ، لَا إِلَهَ إِلَّا اللهُ، وَلَا نَعْبُدُ إِلَّا إِيَّاهُ، لَهُ النِّعْمَةُ وَلَهُ الْفَضْلُ وَلَهُ الثَّنَاءُ الْحَسَنُ، لَا إِلَهَ إِلَّا اللهُ مُخْلِصِينَ لَهُ الدِّينَ وَلَوْ كَرِهَ الْكَافِرُونَ.

Lā ilāha illallāhu waḥdahu lā sharīka lahu, lahul-mulku wa lahul-ḥamdu wa Huwa `alā kulli shay'in Qadīr. Lā ḥawla wa lā quwwata illā billāh. Lā ilāha illallāhu, wa lā na`budu illā iyyāhu, lahun-ni`matu wa lahul-faḍlu wa lahuth-thanā'ul-ḥasanu. Lā ilāha illallāhu mukhliṣīna lahud-dīna wa law karihal-kāfirūn.

None has the right to be worshipped but Allāh alone who has no partner. His is the dominion and to Him belongs all praise; And He has power over all things. There is no power or might except by Allāh. None has the right to be worshipped but Allāh, and we do not worship any other besides Him. Grace and beneficence are His and to Him belongs the most excellent praise. None has the right to be worshipped but Allāh. (We are) sincere in making our religious devotion to Him, even though the disbelievers may hate it.

BENEFITS

Related by al-Bayhaqī that our Prophet ﷺ said: "For everything there is a polish, and the polish for the hearts is the remembrance of Allāh."

The phrase "*lā ḥawla wa lā quwwata illā billāh*" (There is no power or might except by Allāh.) was described by the Prophet ﷺ as being a treasure from the treasures of Paradise. It reminds us that the ability to do good and stay away from wrong comes from Allāh ﷻ

NOTES

4. Related in Ṣaḥīḥ Muslim

WHAT TO SAY AFTER THE OBLIGATORY PRAYERS

BENEFITS

Imām Muslim ﷺ adds that our Prophet ﷺ said: "Whoever says this after every prayer will be forgiven his sins even if they be like the foam of the sea."

Subḥānallāh means to declare Allāh ﷻ to be free from any imperfection whilst at the same time affirming complete perfection for him.

NOTES

Repeat the ***first phrase 33 times***, and the ***second phrase once***. The total of the individual words of praise become 99, with the second phrase making it 100.

5. Related in Sahīh Muslim

سُبْحَانَ اللهِ، وَالْحَمْدُ للهِ، وَاللهُ أَكْبَرُ.

Subḥānallāhi, walḥamdu lillāhi wallāhu akbar.

How perfect Allāh is, all praise be to Allāh , and Allāh is the Greatest.

لَا إِلَهَ إِلَّا اللهُ وَحْدَهُ لَا شَرِيكَ لَهُ، لَهُ الْمُلْكُ وَلَهُ الْحَمْدُ وَهُوَ عَلَى كُلِّ شَيْءٍ قَدِيرٌ.

Lā ilāha illallāhu waḥdahu lā sharīka lah, lahul-mulku wa lahul-ḥamdu wa Huwa `alā kulli shay'in Qadīr.

None has the right to be worshipped but Allāh alone who has no partner. His is the dominion and to Him belongs all praise; And He has power over all things.

WHAT TO SAY AFTER THE OBLIGATORY PRAYERS

بِسۡمِ ٱللَّهِ ٱلرَّحۡمَٰنِ ٱلرَّحِيمِ
قُلۡ أَعُوذُ بِرَبِّ ٱلۡفَلَقِ ١ مِن شَرِّ مَا خَلَقَ ٢
وَمِن شَرِّ غَاسِقٍ إِذَا وَقَبَ ٣ وَمِن شَرِّ ٱلنَّفَّٰثَٰتِ
فِي ٱلۡعُقَدِ ٤ وَمِن شَرِّ حَاسِدٍ إِذَا حَسَدَ ٥

Bismillāhir-Raḥmānir-Raḥīm.
"Qul a`ūdhū birabbil-falaq.
Min sharri mā khalaq.
Wa min sharri ghāsiqin idhā waqab.
Wa min sharrin-naffāthāti fil-`ūqad.
Wa min sharri ḥāsidin idhā ḥasad."

With the Name of Allāh, the All Merciful, the Most Merciful.
"Say: I take refuge with the Lord of daybreak,
from the evil of what He created,
from the evil of darkness as it envelops,
from the evil of those who blow on knots,
and from the evil of an envier when he envies."
(al-Falaq 113:1-5)

Continued onto next page

BENEFITS

Ibn al-Qayyim رَحِمَهُ ٱللَّهُ said: "Remembrance endows a person with love which is the very spirit of Islām, the pivotal point of religion and the axis of eternal happiness and deliverance."

Seeking refuge in Allāh عَزَّ وَجَلَّ is a mark of servitude because it reflects a dire state of need for Allāh عَزَّ وَجَلَّ

BENEFITS

The Prophet ﷺ said: "If your hearts were always in the state that they are in during dhikr, the angels would come to see you to the point that they would greet you in the middle of the road." Narrated by Imām Muslim.

بِسۡمِ ٱللَّهِ ٱلرَّحۡمَٰنِ ٱلرَّحِيمِ
قُلۡ أَعُوذُ بِرَبِّ ٱلنَّاسِ ١ مَلِكِ ٱلنَّاسِ ٢ إِلَٰهِ
ٱلنَّاسِ ٣ مِن شَرِّ ٱلۡوَسۡوَاسِ ٱلۡخَنَّاسِ ٤ ٱلَّذِي
يُوَسۡوِسُ فِي صُدُورِ ٱلنَّاسِ ٥ مِنَ ٱلۡجِنَّةِ وَٱلنَّاسِ
٦

Bismillāhir-Raḥmānir-Raḥīm.
"Qul a`ūdhū birabbin-nās.
Malikin-nās. Ilāhin-nās.
Min sharril-waswāsil-khannās.
Alladhī yuwaswisu fī ṣudūrin-nās.
Minal-jinnati wannās."

With the Name of Allāh, the All Merciful, the Most Merciful.
"Say: I take refuge with the Lord of mankind, the King of mankind, the God of mankind, from the evil of the Stealthy Whisperer, who whispers in people's breasts, (coming) from the jinn and man."
(al-Nās 114:1-6)

NOTES

These two sūrahs are to be recited *once after each obligatory prayer* and *three times after Fajr & Maghrib.*

6. Related in the Sunans of Abū Dāwūd, al-Tirmidhī & al-Nasā'ī

WHAT TO SAY AFTER THE OBLIGATORY PRAYERS

ٱللَّهُ لَآ إِلَٰهَ إِلَّا هُوَ ٱلۡحَيُّ ٱلۡقَيُّومُۚ لَا تَأۡخُذُهُۥ سِنَةٞ
وَلَا نَوۡمٞۚ لَّهُۥ مَا فِي ٱلسَّمَٰوَٰتِ وَمَا فِي ٱلۡأَرۡضِۗ مَن ذَا
ٱلَّذِي يَشۡفَعُ عِندَهُۥٓ إِلَّا بِإِذۡنِهِۦۚ يَعۡلَمُ مَا بَيۡنَ أَيۡدِيهِمۡ
وَمَا خَلۡفَهُمۡۖ وَلَا يُحِيطُونَ بِشَيۡءٖ مِّنۡ عِلۡمِهِۦٓ إِلَّا بِمَا
شَآءَۚ وَسِعَ كُرۡسِيُّهُ ٱلسَّمَٰوَٰتِ وَٱلۡأَرۡضَۖ وَلَا يَـُٔودُهُۥ
حِفۡظُهُمَاۚ وَهُوَ ٱلۡعَلِيُّ ٱلۡعَظِيمُ ٢٥٥

Allāhu lā ilāha illā Huwal-Ḥayyul-Qayyūm, lā ta'khudhuhū sinatun wa lā nawm, lahū māfis-samāwāti wa mā fīl-arḍ, man dhal-ladhī yashfa`u `indahū illā bi idhnihī, ya`lamu mābayna aydīhim wa mā khalfahum, wa lā yuḥīṭūna bishay'im-min `ilmihī illā bi mā shā'a, wasi`a kursiyyuhus-samāwāti wal arḍ, wa lā ya'ūduhu hifẓuhumā, wa Huwal-`Aliyyul-`Aẓīm.

Allāh, there is none worthy of worship save Him, the Living, the Sustainer. He is not subject to drowsiness or sleep. Everything in the heavens and the earth belongs to Him. Who can intercede with Him except by His permission?
He knows what is before them and what is behind them but they cannot grasp any of His knowledge save what He wills. His Footstool encompasses the heavens and the earth and their preservation does not tire Him. He is the Most High,
the Magnificent.
(al-Baqarah 2:255)

BENEFITS

This is the greatest āyah in the Noble Qur'ān known as the Verse of the Footstool – Āyatul-Kursī (al-Baqarah 2:255)

The narration of Imām al-Nasā'ī adds, "Nothing stops a person who recites this verse from entering paradise except death."

NOTES

7. Related by Sunan al-Nasā'ī

BENEFITS

Mu'ādh ibn Jabal said that the Prophet ﷺ said: "The People of Paradise will not regret except one thing alone: the hour that passed them by and in which they made no remembrance of Allāh." Narrated in the Sunan of al-Bayhaqī and al-Ṭabarānī.

NOTES

Recite *ten times after Fajr and Maghrib* prayers.

8. Related in the Sunan al-Tirmidhī & Musnad Aḥmad)

لَا إِلَٰهَ إِلَّا اللهُ وَحْدَهُ لَا شَرِيكَ لَهُ، لَهُ الْمُلْكُ وَلَهُ الْحَمْدُ يُحْيِي وَيُمِيتُ، وَهُوَ عَلَى كُلِّ شَيْءٍ قَدِيرٌ.

Lā ilāha illallāhu waḥdahu lā sharīka lahu, lahul-mulku wa lahul-ḥamdu yuḥyī wa yumītu wa Huwa `alā kulli shay'in Qadīr.

None has the right to be worshipped but Allāh alone who has no partner. His is the dominion and to Him belongs all praise. He gives life and He causes death; And He has power over all things.

WHAT TO SAY IN THE MORNINGS & EVENINGS

Anas ﷺ said that he heard the Prophet ﷺ say: "Sitting with people remembering Allāh, Most High, from the morning (Fajr) prayer until sunrise is more beloved to me than freeing four slaves from the Children of Ismā'īl. Sitting with people remembering Allāh from the afternoon (`Aṣr) prayer until the sun sets is more beloved to me than freeing four slaves from the Children of Ismā'īl."

Related in Sunan Abū Dāwūd

In this section the words of rememberance and supplication are for both the morning and evening and should be recited in Arabic and once only unless otherwise stated. Some supplications have seperate wordings for mornings and evenings as has been indicated.

The morning referred to, is from dawn-break up to when the Sun has risen at the forenoon this may further be extended to the noon prayer. The best time for the evening remembrances is from the 'Asr prayer until the Sun has set with the time extended to reaching the first part of the night.

BENEFITS

The Prophet ﷺ said: "Whoever says this when he rises in the morning will be protected from the jinn until he retires in the evening, and whoever says it when retiring in the evening will be protected from them until he rises in the morning."

This noble verse establishes the greatness of Allāh ﷻ. The greatness of the verse stems from the numerous names & attributes of Allāh ﷻ that are mentioned. This fact alone merits contemplation.

NOTES

1. Related in Mustadraq al-Ḥākim)

ٱللَّهُ لَآ إِلَـٰهَ إِلَّا هُوَ ٱلْحَىُّ ٱلْقَيُّومُ ۚ لَا تَأْخُذُهُۥ سِنَةٌ وَلَا نَوْمٌ ۚ لَّهُۥ مَا فِى ٱلسَّمَـٰوَٰتِ وَمَا فِى ٱلْأَرْضِ ۗ مَن ذَا ٱلَّذِى يَشْفَعُ عِندَهُۥٓ إِلَّا بِإِذْنِهِۦ ۚ يَعْلَمُ مَا بَيْنَ أَيْدِيهِمْ وَمَا خَلْفَهُمْ ۖ وَلَا يُحِيطُونَ بِشَىْءٍ مِّنْ عِلْمِهِۦٓ إِلَّا بِمَا شَآءَ ۚ وَسِعَ كُرْسِيُّهُ ٱلسَّمَـٰوَٰتِ وَٱلْأَرْضَ ۖ وَلَا يَـُٔودُهُۥ حِفْظُهُمَا ۚ وَهُوَ ٱلْعَلِىُّ ٱلْعَظِيمُ ﴿٢٥٥﴾

Allāhu lā ilāha illā Huwal-Ḥayyul-Qayyūm, lā ta'khudhuhū sinatun wa lā nawm, lahū māfis-samāwāti wa mā fīl-arḍ, man dhal-ladhī yashfa`u `indahū illā bi idhnihī, ya`lamu mābayna aydīhim wa mā khalfahum, wa lā yuḥīṭūna bishay'im-min `ilmihī illā bi mā shā'a, wasi`a kursiyyuhus-samāwāti wal arḍ, wa lā ya'ūduhu hifẓuhumā, wa Huwal-`Aliyyul-`Aẓīm.

Allāh, there is none worthy of worship save Him, the Living, the Sustainer. He is not subject to drowsiness or sleep. Everything in the heavens and the earth belongs to Him. Who can intercede with Him except by His permission?
He knows what is before them and what is behind them but they cannot grasp any of His knowledge save what He wills. His Footstool encompasses the heavens and the earth and their preservation does not tire Him. He is the Most High, the Magnificent.
(al-Baqarah 2:255)

بِسۡمِ ٱللَّهِ ٱلرَّحۡمَٰنِ ٱلرَّحِيمِ
قُلۡ هُوَ ٱللَّهُ أَحَدٌ ١ ٱللَّهُ ٱلصَّمَدُ ٢
لَمۡ يَلِدۡ وَلَمۡ يُولَدۡ ٣ وَلَمۡ يَكُن لَّهُۥ كُفُوًا أَحَدُۢ ٤

Bismillāhir-Raḥmānir-Raḥīm.
"Qul Huwallāhu Aḥad.
Allāhus-Ṣamad.
Lam yalid wa lam yūlad.
Wa lam yakun lahū kufuwan aḥad"

With the Name of Allāh, the All Merciful, the Most Merciful. "Say: He is Allāh, the One and only. Allāh, the Everlasting Sustainer of all. He fathered none, nor was He born. And no one is comparable to Him."
(al-Ikhlāṣ 112:1-4)

Continued onto next page

BENEFITS

The Prophet ﷺ said: "Say: He is Allāh, the One and al-Mu'awwidhatayn (i.e., Sūrahs al-Falaq and al-Nās) ***in the evening and in the morning, three times***, and that will suffice you against everything." Related in Sunan al-Nasā'ī

Sūrah al-Ikhlāṣ equates to a third of the Qur'ān.

Allāh ﷻ has created all things in pairs to illustrate the need they have for one another. Allāh ﷻ on the other hand, is One and is in no need of anything, whereas we are in need of him.

NOTES

2. Related in Sunan Abū Dāwūd & Musnad Aḥmad

BENEFITS

Reciting these verses every day in the morning and evening upon ourselves and our children is one of the best means of protection from the evils surrounding us.

بِسۡمِ ٱللَّهِ ٱلرَّحۡمَٰنِ ٱلرَّحِيمِ
قُلۡ أَعُوذُ بِرَبِّ ٱلۡفَلَقِ ١ مِن شَرِّ مَا خَلَقَ ٢ وَمِن
شَرِّ غَاسِقٍ إِذَا وَقَبَ ٣ وَمِن شَرِّ ٱلنَّفَّٰثَٰتِ فِي
ٱلۡعُقَدِ ٤ وَمِن شَرِّ حَاسِدٍ إِذَا حَسَدَ ٥

Bismillāhir-Raḥmānir-Raḥīm.
"Qul a`ūdhu birabbil-falaq.
Min sharri mā khalaq.
Wa min sharri ghāsiqin idhā waqab.
Wa min sharrin-naffāthāti fil-`ūqad.
Wa min sharri ḥāsidin idhā ḥasad."

With the Name of Allāh, the All Merciful,
the Most Merciful.
"Say: I take refuge with the Lord of daybreak,
from the evil of what He created,
from the evil of darkness as it envelops,
from the evil of those who blow on knots,
and from the evil of an envier when he envies."
(al-Falaq 113:1-5)

بِسْمِ ٱللَّهِ ٱلرَّحْمَٰنِ ٱلرَّحِيمِ
قُلْ أَعُوذُ بِرَبِّ ٱلنَّاسِ ﴿١﴾ مَلِكِ ٱلنَّاسِ ﴿٢﴾ إِلَٰهِ
ٱلنَّاسِ ﴿٣﴾ مِن شَرِّ ٱلْوَسْوَاسِ ٱلْخَنَّاسِ ﴿٤﴾ ٱلَّذِى
يُوَسْوِسُ فِى صُدُورِ ٱلنَّاسِ ﴿٥﴾ مِنَ ٱلْجِنَّةِ وَٱلنَّاسِ ﴿٦﴾

Bismillāhir-Raḥmānir-Raḥīm.
"Qul a`ūdhū birabbin-nās.
Malikin-nās. Ilāhin-nās.
Min sharril-waswāsil-khannās.
Alladhī yuwaswisu fī ṣudūrin-nās.
Minal-jinnati wannās."

With the Name of Allāh, the All Merciful, the Most Merciful.
"Say: I take refuge with the Lord of mankind, the King of mankind, the God of mankind, from the evil of the Stealthy Whisperer, who whispers in people's breasts,

BENEFITS

Ibn al-Qayyim رَحِمَهُ ٱللَّهُ said: "These two chapters are of immense benefit and every single servant is in need of them, and this need is essential and indispensable. They have a potent effect in repressing magic, the evil eye and indeed every form of evil. The need that a servant has for these two chapters is greater than the need he has for rest, food, drink and clothes."

BENEFITS

Ibn al-Qayyim رَحِمَهُ ٱللَّهُ said: "Remembrance strengthens both heart and body. Remembrance brings provision."

NOTES

This wording is for *mornings*

أَصْبَحْنَا وَأَصْبَحَ الْمُلْكُ لِلَّهِ وَالْحَمْدُ لِلَّهِ، لَا إِلَهَ إِلَّا اللهُ وَحْدَهُ لَا شَرِيكَ لَهُ، لَهُ الْمُلْكُ وَلَهُ الْحَمْدُ وَهُوَ عَلَى كُلِّ شَيْءٍ قَدِيرٌ، ربِّ أَسْأَلُكَ خَيْرَ مَا فِي هَذَا الْيَومِ وَخَيْرَ مَا بَعْدَهُ، وَأَعُوذُ بِكَ مِنْ شَرِّ مَا فِي هَذَا الْيَومِ وَشَرِّ مَا بَعْدَهُ، رَبِّ أَعُوذُ بِكَ مِنَ الْكَسَلِ، وَسُوءِ الكِبَرِ، رَبِّ أَعُوذُ بِكَ مِنْ عَذَابٍ فِي النَّارِ وَعَذَابٍ فِي الْقَبْرِ.

Aṣbaḥnā wa aṣbaḥal-mulku lillāhi wal-ḥamdu lillāhi, lā ilāha illallāhu waḥdahu lā sharīka lahu, lahul-mulku wa lahul-ḥamdu wa Huwa `alā kulli shay'in Qadīr. Rabbi as'aluka khayra mā fī hādhal-yawmi wa khayra mā ba`dahū wa a`ūdhu bika min sharri mā fī hādhal-yawmi wa sharri mā ba`dahū, Rabbi a`ūdhu bika minal-kasali, wa sū'il-kibari, Rabbi a`ūdhu bika min `adhābin fin-nāri wa `adhābin fil-qabri.

We have started a new day and with it all dominion is Allāh's. Praise be to Allāh, none has the right to be worshipped but Allāh alone who has no partner. To Allāh belongs the dominion, and to Him belongs all praise; He has power over all things. My Lord, I ask You for the good in this day and the days that come after it, and I take refuge in You from the evil in this day and the days that come after it. My Lord, I take refuge in You from laziness and helpless old age. My Lord, I take refuge in You from the punishment of the Fire, and from the punishment of the grave.

أَمْسَيْنَا وَأَمْسَى الْمُلْكُ لِلّهِ وَالْحَمْدُ لِلّهِ، لا إِلَهَ إِلَّا اللّهُ وَحْدَهُ لَا شَرِيكَ لَهُ، لَهُ الْمُلْكُ وَلَهُ الْحَمْدُ وَهُوَ عَلَى كُلِّ شَيْءٍ قَدِيرٌ، ربِّ أَسْأَلُكَ خَيْرَ مَا فِي هَذِهِ اللَّيْلَةِ وَخَيْرَ مَا بَعْدَهَا، وَأَعُوذُ بِكَ مِنْ شَرِّ مَا فِي هَذِهِ اللَّيْلَةِ وَشَرِّ مَا بَعْدَهَا، رَبِّ أَعُوذُ بِكَ مِنَ الْكَسَلِ، وَسُوءِ الْكِبَرِ، رَبِّ أَعُوذُ بِكَ مِنْ عَذَابٍ فِي النَّارِ وَعَذَابٍ فِي الْقَبْرِ.

Amsaynā wa amsal-mulku lillāh wal-ḥamdu lillāhi, lā ilāha illallāhu waḥdahū lā sharīka lahū, lahul-mulku wa lahul-ḥamdu wa Huwa `alā kulli shay'in Qadīr. Rabbi as'aluka khayra mā fī hādhihil-laylati, wa khayra mā ba`dahā, wa a`ūdhu bika min sharri mā fī hādhihil-laylati wa sharri mā ba`dahā, Rabbi a`ūdhu bika minal-kasali, wa sū'il-kibari, Rabbi a`ūdhu bika min `adhābin fin-nāri wa `adhābin fil-qabri.

We have entered the evening and with it all dominion is Allāh's. Praise be to Allāh, none has the right to be worshipped but Allāh alone who has no partner. To Allāh belongs the dominion, and to Him belongs all praise; He has power over all things. My Lord, I ask you for the good in this night and the nights that come after it and I take refuge in you from the evil in this night and the nights that come after it. My Lord, I take refuge in You from laziness and helpless old age. My Lord, I take refuge in You from the punishment of the Fire, and from the punishment of the grave.

BENEFITS

Our Prophet ﷺ said: "There is nothing more noble than supplication in Allāh's sight." Recorded in Sunan al-Tirmidhī.

NOTES

This wording is for ***evenings***

3. Related in Ṣaḥīḥ Muslim

NOTES

This wording is for *mornings*

اللَّهُمَّ بِكَ أَصْبَحْنَا، وَبِكَ أَمْسَيْنَا، وَبِكَ نَحْيَا، وَبِكَ نَمُوتُ وَإِلَيْكَ النُّشُورُ.

Allāhumma bika aṣbaḥnā, wa bika aṣbaḥnā, wa bika naḥyā, wa bika namūtu wa ilaykan-nushūr.

O Allāh, by You we enter the morning and by You we enter the evening, by You we live and by You we die,

NOTES

This wording is for *evenings*

اللَّهُمَّ بِكَ أَمْسَيْنَا، وَبِكَ أَصْبَحْنَا، وَبِكَ نَحْيَا، وَبِكَ نَمُوتُ وَإِلَيْكَ الْمَصِيرُ.

Allāhumma bika amsaynā, wa bika amsaynā, wa bika naḥyā, wa bika namūtu wa ilaykal-maṣir.

O Allāh, by You we enter the evening and by You we enter the morning, by You we live and by You we die, and to You is the Final Return.

[5]

اللَّهُمَّ أَنْتَ رَبِّي لاَ إِلَهَ إِلَّا أَنْتَ، خَلَقْتَنِي
وَأَنَا عَبْدُكَ، وَأَنَا عَلَى عَهْدِكَ وَوَعْدِكَ مَا
اسْتَطَعْتُ، أَعُوذُ بِكَ مِنْ شَرِّ مَا صَنَعْتُ،
أَبُوءُ لَكَ بِنِعْمَتِكَ عَلَيَّ، وَأَبُوءُ بِذَنْبِي فَاغْفِرْ لِي
فَإِنَّهُ لاَ يَغْفِرُ الذُّنُوبَ إِلَّا أَنْتَ.

Allāhumma Anta Rabbī lā ilāha illā Anta, khalaqtanī wa anā `abduka, wa anā `alā `ahdika wa wa`dika mastaṭa`tu, a`ūdhu bika min sharri mā ṣana`tu, abū'u laka bi ni`matika `alayya, wa abū'u bidhanbī faghfir lī fainnahū lā yaghfirudh-dhunūba illā Anta.

O Allāh, You are my Lord, there is none worthy of worship but You. You created me and I am your slave. I keep to Your covenant and my pledge to You as much as I can. I take refuge in You from the evil of what I have done. I acknowledge Your blessings upon me and I admit my sins. Forgive me, for there is none who forgives sins besides You.

BENEFITS

The Prophet ﷺ declared these words to be the best with which one could seek forgiveness.
He also said in the same ḥadīth: "He who says this during the day with firm belief in it and dies on the same day (before the evening), he will be one of the dwellers of Jannah and if anyone says this during the night with firm belief in it and dies before the morning, he will be from the dwellers of Jannah."

Acknowledging one's shortcomings whilst recognising the greatness of Allāh ﷻ is the basis of being a true slave to Him ﷻ

NOTES

5. Related in Ṣaḥīḥ al-Bukhārī

BENEFITS

Imām al-Bukhārī ﷺ, in his great work al-Adab al-Mufrad adds that the Prophet ﷺ said, "Allāh will spare whoever says this *four times in the morning or evening* from the fire of Hell."

اللَّهُمَّ إِنِّي أَصْبَحْتُ أُشْهِدُكَ وَأُشْهِدُ حَمَلَةَ عَرْشِكَ، وَمَلَائِكَتَكَ وَجَمِيعَ خَلْقِكَ، أَنَّكَ أَنْتَ اللهُ لَا إِلَهَ إِلَّا أَنْتَ وَحْدَكَ لَا شَرِيكَ لَكَ، وَأَنَّ مُحَمَّداً عَبْدُكَ وَرَسُولُكَ.

Allāhumma innī aṣbaḥtu ush-hiduka wa ush-hidu ḥamalata `arshika, wa malā'ikataka wa jamī`a khalqika, annaka Antallāhu lā ilāha illā Anta waḥdaka lā sharīka laka, wa anna Muḥammadan `abduka wa Rasūluka.

O Allāh, I have entered a new morning calling upon You to bear witness, as well as calling to witness the bearers of Your Throne, Your angels and all Your creation that You are Allāh, there is none worthy of worship but You alone, You have no partners, and that Muḥammad is Your servant and Messenger.

NOTES

This wording is for *mornings.*

Recite *four times*

B

اللَّهُمَّ إِنِّي أَمْسَيْتُ أُشْهِدُكَ وَأُشْهِدُ حَمَلَةَ عَرْشِكَ، وَمَلَائِكَتَكَ وَجَمِيعَ خَلْقِكَ، أَنَّكَ أَنْتَ اللهُ لَا إِلَهَ إِلَّا أَنْتَ وَحْدَكَ لَا شَرِيكَ لَكَ، وَأَنَّ مُحَمَّداً عَبْدُكَ وَرَسُولُكَ.

Allāhumma innī amsaytu ush-hiduka wa ush-hidu ḥamalata `arshika, wa malā'ikataka wa jamī`a khalqika, annaka Antallāhu lā ilāha illā Anta waḥdaka lā sharīka laka, wa anna Muḥammadan `abduka wa Rasūluka.

O Allāh, I have entered a new evening calling upon You to bear witness, as well as calling to witness the bearers of Your Throne, Your angels and all Your creation that You are Allāh, there is none worthy of worship but You alone, You have no partners, and that Muḥammad is Your servant and Messenger.

BENEFITS

Ibn al-Qayyim رَحِمَهُ ٱللَّٰهُ reported that he heard Shaykh al-Islām Ibn Taymiyyah رَحِمَهُ ٱللَّٰهُ say: "In this world there is a paradise, whoever does not enter it will not enter the Paradise of the Hereafter."

NOTES

This wording is for *evenings*

Recite *four times*

6. Related in Sunan Abū Dāwūd

7 اللَّهُمَّ مَا أَصْبَحَ بِي مِنْ نِعْمَةٍ أَوْ بِأَحَدٍ مِنْ خَلْقِكَ فَمِنْكَ وَحْدَكَ لَا شَرِيكَ لَكَ، فَلَكَ الْحَمْدُ وَلَكَ الشُّكْرُ.

Allāhumma mā aṣbaḥa biya min ni`matin aw bi aḥadin min khalqika faminka waḥdaka lā sharīka laka, falakal-ḥamdu wa lakash-shukru.

O Allāh, whatever blessing I have or any one of Your creatures has on this morning is from You alone, You have no partner. So all praise is for You and gratitude is due to You.

7 اللَّهُمَّ مَا أَمْسَى بِي مِنْ نِعْمَةٍ أَوْ بِأَحَدٍ مِنْ خَلْقِكَ فَمِنْكَ وَحْدَكَ لَا شَرِيكَ لَكَ، فَلَكَ الْحَمْدُ وَلَكَ الشُّكْرُ.

Allāhumma mā amsā biya min ni`matin aw bi aḥadin min khalqika faminka waḥdaka lā sharīka laka, falakal-ḥamdu walakash-shukru.

O Allāh, whatever blessing I have or any one of Your creatures has on this evening is from You alone, You have no partner. So all praise is for You and gratitude is due to You.

BENEFITS

The Prophet ﷺ informed us that whoever says this in the morning has offered gratitude for his day and whoever says this in the evening has offered gratitude for his night.

True gratitude stems from the heart through recognising that all blessings are from Him ﷻ alone.

NOTES

7a. This wording is for ***mornings***.

7b. This wording is for ***evenings***.

7. Related in Sunan Abū Dāwūd

اللَّهُمَّ عافِـني في بَدَني، اللَّهُمَّ عافِـني في سَمْـعي، اللّهُـمَّ عافِـني في بَصَـرِي، لا إلهَ إلاّ أَنْـتَ.

اللّهُـمَّ إِنّـي أَعـوذُ بِكَ مِنَ الْكُـفر، وَالفَـقْر، اللّهُـمَّ إِنّـي أَعـوذُ بِكَ مِنْ عَذابِ القَـبْر، لا إلهَ إلاّ أَنْـتَ.

Allāhumma `āfinī fī badanī, Allāhumma `āfinī fī sam`ī, Allāhumma `āfinī fī baṣarī, lā ilāha illā Anta.

Allāhumma innī a`ūdhu bika minal-kufri, wal-faqri, Allāhumma innī a`ūdhu bika min `adhābil-qabri, lā ilāha illā Anta.

O Allāh, grant my body good health. O Allāh, preserve my hearing for me. O Allāh, preserve my sight for me. There is none worthy of worship but You.

O Allāh, I take refuge in You from disbelief and poverty, O Allāh, I take refuge in You from the punishment of the grave. There is none worthy of worship but You.

BENEFITS

Abu Bakrah ﷺ, said: "I heard the Prophet ﷺ supplicate with these words and I love to adopt his sunnah as something to emulate."

A believer should never feel complacent about his faith and should fear that he may fall into misguidance.

NOTES

Repeat *first part of the supplication three times.* Then repeat the *second part three times.*

8. Related in Sunan Abū Dāwūd & Musnad Aḥmad

BENEFITS

The Companion Abū al-Dardā' ﷺ, said: "Whoever says this *in the morning and evening seven times,* Allāh will suffice him all his needs."

حَسْبِيَ اللهُ لَا إِلَهَ إِلَّا هُوَ عَلَيْهِ تَوَكَّلْتُ وَهُوَ رَبُّ الْعَرْشِ الْعَظِيمِ.

Ḥasbiyallāhu lā ilāha illā Huwa `alayhi tawakkaltu wa Huwa Rabbul -`Arshil -`Aẓīm.

Allāh is sufficient for me. There is none worthy of worship but Him. I have placed my trust in Him, And He is Lord of the Majestic Throne.

NOTES

Repeat *seven times.*

9. Related in Sunan Abū Dāwūd

اللَّهُمَّ إِنِّي أَسْأَلُكَ الْعَفْوَ وَالْعَافِيَةَ فِي الدُّنْيَا وَالآخِرَةِ، اللَّهُمَّ إِنِّي أَسْأَلُكَ الْعَفْوَ وَالْعَافِيَةَ فِي دِينِي وَدُنْيَايَ وَأَهْلِي وَمَالِي،اللَّهُمَّ اسْتُرْ عَوْرَاتِي، وَآمِنْ رَوْعَاتِي،

اللَّهُمَّ احْفَظْنِي مِنْ بَيْنِ يَدَيَّ، وَمِنْ خَلْفِي، وَعَنْ يَمِينِي، وَعَنْ شِمَالِي، وَمِنْ فَوْقِي، وَأَعُوذُ بِعَظَمَتِكَ أَنْ أُغْتَالَ مِنْ تَحْتِي.

Allāhumma innī as'alukal-`afwa wal `āfiyata fid-dunyā wal ākhirati, Allāhumma innī as'alukal-`afwa wal `āfiyata fī dīnī wa dunyāya wa ahlī wa mālī. Allāhum-mastur `awrātī, wa āmin raw`ātī. Allāhum-maḥfaẓnī min bayni yadayya, wa min khalfī, wa `an yamīnī, wa `an shimālī, wa min fawqī, wa a`ūdhu bi `aẓamatika an ughtāla min taḥtī.

O Allāh, I ask for Your pardon and well-being in this world and the next. O Allāh, I ask for Your pardon and soundness in my religion, my worldly affairs, my family and my wealth.
O Allāh, conceal my shame and protect me from anguish. O Allāh, guard me from what is before me, behind me, my left, my right and above me. I take refuge in Your greatness against being struck down from beneath me.

BENEFITS

The Prophet ﷺ said: "The earth and everything in it is cursed, except for dhikr and what follows on from it, and a teacher and a student." Narrated by Imām al Tirmidhī.

The dhikr mentioned here is general covering words of remmeberance; supplication; reading Qur'ān; speaking the truth; enjoing the good and forbiding evil; learning and teaching the affairs of the religion etc.

NOTES

10. Related in Sunan Abū Dāwūd & Sunan Ibn Mājah

BENEFITS

Ibn al-Qayyim رَحِمَهُ ٱللَّٰهُ said: "Remembrance adorns the one who practices it with dignity, sweetness and radiance."

اللَّهُمَّ عَالِمَ الْغَيْبِ وَالشَّهَادَةِ فَاطِرَ السَّمَاوَاتِ وَالْأَرْضِ، رَبَّ كُلِّ شَيْءٍ وَمَلِيكَهُ، أَشْهَدُ أَنْ لَا إِلَهَ إِلَّا أَنْتَ، أَعُوذُ بِكَ مِنْ شَرِّ نَفْسِي، وَمِنْ شَرِّ الشَّيْطَانِ وَشِرْكِهِ، وَأَنْ أَقْتَرِفَ عَلَى نَفْسِي سُوءاً، أَوْ أَجُرَّهُ إِلَى مُسْلِمٍ.

Allāhumma `Ālimal-ghaybi wash-shahādati fāṭiras-samāwāti wal arḍi, Rabba kulli shay'in wa malīkahu, ash-hadu an lā ilāha illā Anta, a`ūdhu bika min sharri nafsī, wa min sharrish-shayṭāni wa shirkihi, wa an aqtarifa `alā nafsī sū'an, aw ajurrahu ilā Muslimin.

O Allāh, Knower of the unseen and the seen, Originator of the heavens and the earth, Lord of everything and its owner; I bear witness that there is none worthy of worship but You. I take refuge in You from the evil of my soul and from the evil of Satan and his (inciting towards) shirk. (I take refuge in You) from bringing evil upon my soul or harming any Muslim.

NOTES

11. Related in Sunan Abū Dāwūd & Sunan al-Tirmidhī

بِسْمِ اللهِ الَّذِي لَا يَضُرُّ مَعَ اسْمِهِ شَيْءٌ فِي الْأَرْضِ وَلَا فِي السَّمَاءِ وَهُوَ السَّمِيعُ الْعَلِيمُ.

Bismillāhil-ladhī lā yaḍurru ma`as-mihī shay'un fil-arḍi wa lā fis-samā'i wa Huwas-Samī`ul - `Alīm.

In the Name of Allāh with whose Name nothing can cause harm, neither in the earth nor in the heavens. He is the All-Hearing, the All-Knowing.

BENEFITS

12. The Prophet ﷺ said: "Whoever recites it ***three times in the morning*** will not be afflicted by any calamity before evening, and whoever recites it ***three times in the evening*** will not be overtaken by any calamity before morning."

رَضِيتُ بِاللهِ رَبّاً، وَبِالْإِسْلَامِ دِيناً، وَبِمُحَمَّدٍ صَلَّى اللهُ عَلَيْهِ وَسَلَّمَ نَبِيّاً.

Raḍītu billāhi Rabban, wa bil-Islāmi dīnan, wa bi Muḥammadin ṣallallāhu `alayhi wa sallam Nabiyyan.

I am pleased with Allāh as my Lord, with Islām as my religion and with Muḥammad ﷺ as my Prophet.

13. "Allāh has promised that anyone who says this ***three times every morning or evening*** will be pleased on the Day of Rising."

NOTES

12. Related in Sunan Abū Dāwūd & Sunan al-Tirmidhī

13. Related in Sunan al-Tirmidhī & Musnad Aḥmad

يَا حَيُّ يَا قَيُّومُ بِرَحْمَتِكَ أَسْتَغِيثُ أَصْلِحْ لِي شَأْنِي كُلَّهُ وَلَا تَكِلْنِي إِلَى نَفْسِي طَرْفَةَ عَيْنٍ.

Yā Ḥayyu yā Qayyūmu biraḥmatika astaghīthu aṣliḥ lī sha'nī kullahu wa lā takilnī ilā nafsī ṭarfata `aynin.

O Ever Living One, O Sustainer One,
by Your mercy do I ask for Your support in setting all my affairs right. Do not leave me to my soul for so much as the blink of an eye.

BENEFITS

Ibn al-Qayyim رحمه الله said : "Remembrance endows one with vigilance (al-murāqabah), which opens the door of self reform. Entering it, the servant worships Allāh as if he were seeing Him. There is no way for the heedless man to reach the station of excellence (iḥsān), any more than for a seated man to reach his home

NOTES

14. Related in Sunan al-Nasā'ī & Mustadrak al-Ḥākim

لَا إِلَهَ إِلَّا اللهُ وَحْدَهُ لَا شَرِيكَ لَهُ، لَهُ الْمُلْكُ وَلَهُ الْحَمْدُ، وَهُوَ عَلَى كُلِّ شَيْءٍ قَدِيرٌ.

Lā ilāha illallāhu waḥdahū lā sharīka lahū, lahul-mulku wa lahul-ḥamdu, wa Huwa `alā kulli shay'in Qadīr.

None has the right to be worshipped but Allāh alone who has no partner. His is the dominion and to Him belongs all praise; He has power over all things.

BENEFITS

15. "Allāh ﷻ will record one hundred good deeds for whoever says this ***ten times*** in the morning, and forgive him one hundred sins. He will have the reward of freeing a slave and will be protected from Satan throughout the day until dusk. Whoever says it in the evening will have the same reward."

"...or at least ***once***."

سُبْحَانَ اللهِ وَبِحَمْدِهِ عَدَدَ خَلْقِهِ، وَرِضَا نَفْسِهِ، وَزِنَةَ عَرْشِهِ وَمِدَادَ كَلِمَاتِهِ.

Subḥānallāhi wa biḥamdihī `adada khalqihī, wa riḍā nafsihī, wa zinata `arshihī wa midāda kalimātihī.

How perfect Allāh is and I praise Him by the number of His creation; by His own pleasure; by the weight of His Throne; and by the ink of His words.

16. Recite ***three times*** upon rising in the ***morning only.***

NOTES

15. Related in Musnad Aḥmad

16. Related in Ṣaḥīḥ Muslim

BENEFITS

Allāh ﷻ says: ***"Behold in the Remembrance of Allāh do hearts find tranquillity and satisfaction."*** *(al- Ra'd,13: 28)*

In this world, we should find in the remembrance of Allāh, praising Him and worshipping Him, a delight that is incomparable to anything else.

أَصْبَحْنَا وَأَصْبَحَ الْمُلْكُ لِلَّهِ رَبِّ الْعَالَمِينَ اللَّهُمَّ إِنِّي أَسْأَلُكَ خَيْرَ هَذَا الْيَوْمِ فَتْحَهُ وَنَصْرَهُ وَنُورَهُ وَبَرَكَتَهُ وَهُدَاهُ وَأَعُوذُ بِكَ مِنْ شَرِّ مَا فِيهِ وَشَرِّ مَا بَعْدَهُ.

Aṣbaḥnā wa aṣbaḥal-mulku lillāhi Rabbil-`ālamīn. Allāhumma innī as'aluka khayra hādhal-yawmi: Fatḥahu wa naṣrahu wa nūrahu, wa barakatahu, wa hudāhu, wa a`ūdhu bika min sharri mā fīhi wa sharri mā ba`dahu.

We have started a new day and with it all dominion is Allāh's, Lord of all being. O Allāh, I ask You for the good in this day: its victory, its help, its light, its blessings and its guidance. And I take refuge in You from the evil that is in it and from the evil that follows it.

NOTES

This wording is for ***mornings.***

17. Related in Sunan Abū Dāwūd

أَمْسَيْنَا وَأَمْسَى الْمُلْكُ لِلَّهِ رَبِّ الْعَالَمِينَ اللَّهُمَّ
إِنِّي أَسْأَلُكَ خَيْرَ هَذِهِ اللَّيْلَةِ فَتْحَهَا وَنَصْرَهَا
وَنُورَهَا وَبَرَكَتَهَا وَهُدَاهَا وَأَعُوذُ بِكَ مِنْ شَرِّ مَا
فِيهَا وَشَرِّ مَا بَعْدَهَا.

Amsaynā wa amsal-mulku lillāhi Rabbil-`ālamīn. Allāhumma innī as'aluka khayra hādhihil-laylati: Fatḥahā wanaṣrahā wanūrahā, wabarakatahā, wahudāhā, waa`ūdhubika min sharri mā fīhā washarri mā ba`dahā.

We have started a new night and with it all dominion is Allāh's, Lord of all being. O Allāh, I ask You for the good in this night: its victory, its help, its light, its blessings and its guidance. And I take refuge in You from the evil that is in it and from the evil that follows it.

BENEFITS

The Prophet ﷺ said: "Shall I not inform you of the best of your actions which are the purest to your Lord, which exalt you to the high ranks, which are more efficacious than spending gold and silver (in charity), and better for you than you should encounter your enemies whom you will smite their necks and they will smite your necks?" They said, "Certainly." He ﷺ said, "Remembrance of Allāh the Exalted." Related in Sunan al-Tirmidhī

NOTES

This wording is for ***evenings***.

BENEFITS

The Prophet ﷺ said: "The similitude of one who remembers Allāh and one who does not, is like the similitude of the living and the dead." Related in Ṣaḥīḥ al-Bukhārī & Ṣaḥīḥ Muslim.

أَصْبَحْنَا عَلَى فِطْرَةِ الْإِسْلَامِ وَعَلَى كَلِمَةِ
الْإِخْلَاصِ، وَعَلَى دِينِ نَبِيِّنَا مُحَمَّدٍ صَلَّى اللهُ
عَلَيْهِ وَسَلَّمَ، وَعَلَى مِلَّةِ أَبِينَا إِبْرَاهِيمَ، حَنِيفاً مُسْلِماً
وَمَا كَانَ مِنَ الْمُشْرِكِينَ.

Aṣbaḥnā`alā fiṭratil-Islāmi wa `alā kalimatil-ikhlāṣi, wa `alā dīni Nabiyyinā Muḥammadin (ṣallallāhu `alayhi wa sallama), wa `alā millati abīnā Ibrāhīma, ḥanīfan Musliman wa mā kāna minal-mushrikīn.

We have started a new day upon the natural religion of Islām, the statement of sincerity,
the religion of our Prophet, Muḥammad ﷺ,
and the path of our father, Ibrāhīm. He was upright and devout, and a Muslim. He was never of the polytheists.

NOTES

This wording is for ***mornings.***

18. Related in Sunan al-Tirmidhī & Musnad Aḥmad

أَمْسَيْنَا عَلَى فِطْرَةِ الْإِسْلَامِ وَعَلَى كَلِمَةِ
الْإِخْلَاصِ، وَعَلَى دِينِ نَبِيِّنَا مُحَمَّدٍ صَلَّى اللهُ
عَلَيْهِ وَسَلَّمَ، وَعَلَى مِلَّةِ أَبِينَا إِبْرَاهِيمَ، حَنِيفاً
مُسْلِماً وَمَا كَانَ مِنَ الْمُشْرِكِينَ.

Amsaynā `alā fiṭratil-Islāmi wa `alā kalimatil-ikhlāṣi, wa `alā dīni Nabiyyinā Muḥammadin (ṣallallāhu `alayhi wa sallama), wa `alā millati abīnā Ibrāhīma, ḥanīfan Musliman wa mā kāna minal-mushrikīn.

We start this evening upon the natural religion of Islām, the statement of sincerity, the religion of our Prophet, Muḥammad ﷺ and the path of our father, Ibrāhīm. He was upright and devout, and a Muslim. He was never of the polytheists.

NOTES

This wording is for *evenings*

سُبْحَانَ اللهِ وَبِحَمْدِهِ.

Subḥānallāhi wa biḥamdihī.

How perfect Allāh is and I praise Him.

BENEFITS & NOTES

"Whoever recites this ***one hundred times in the morning and in the evening*** will not be surpassed on the Day of Rising by anyone having done better than this except for someone who had recited it more."

19. Related in Ṣaḥīḥ al-Bukhārī

BENEFITS

20. Recited in the *morning only*

Beneficial knowledge opens the door to good deeds.

اللَّهُمَّ إِنِّي أَسْأَلُكَ عِلْماً نَافِعاً، وَرِزْقاً طَيِّباً، وَعَمَلاً مُتَقَبَّلاً.

Allāhumma innī as'aluka `ilman nāfi`an, wa rizqan ṭayyiban, wa `amalan mutaqabbalan.

O Allāh, I ask You for beneficial knowledge, wholesome provision and deeds that will be accepted.

21. Recite it *one hundred times in the morning only*

أَسْتَغْفِرُ اللهَ.

Astaghfirullāha.

I ask Allāh's forgiveness.

22. "Whoever recites this *three times in the evening* will be protected from insect stings."

أَعُوذُ بِكَلِمَاتِ اللهِ التَّامَّاتِ مِنْ شَرِّ مَا خَلَقَ.

A`ūdhu bikalimātillāhit-tāmmāti min sharri mā khalaqa.

I take refuge in Allāh's Perfect Words from the evil of what He has created.

NOTES

20. Related in Musnad Aḥmad

21. Related by al-Ṭabarānī

22. Related in Musnad Aḥmad & Sunan al-Tirmidhī